Venezuela
Climbing Ilu Tepuy

Stephen and Scharlie Platt

www.leveretpublishing.com

Venezuela: Climbing Ilu Tepuy
First published - August 2013
Second Edition - May 2017
Published by
Leveret Publishing
56 Covent Garden, Cambridge, CB1 2HR, UK

ISBN 978-1-9124600-0-7

© Stephen and Scharlie Platt 2013

All rights reserved. No part of this publication may be reproduced, stored in a retrieval system or transmitted in any form by any means, electronic, mechanical, photocopying, recording or otherwise, except brief extracts for the purpose of review, without the written permission of the publisher.

Ilu Tepuy

Venezuela: Ilu Tepuy 1981

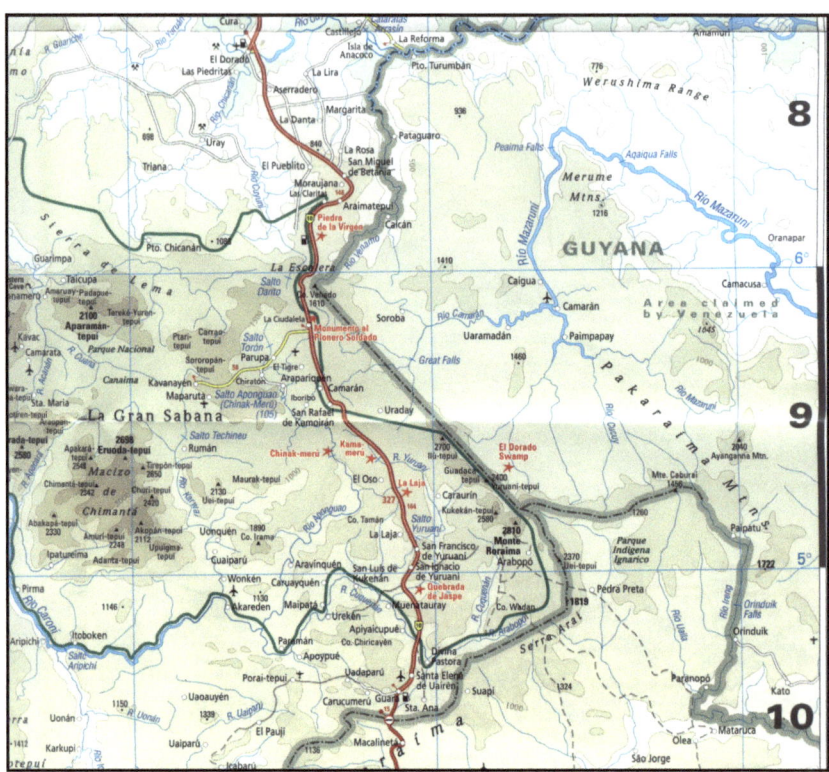

Ilu Tepuy is a sandstone butte 2,700 metres high in the Gran Sabana of Venezuela north-west of Roraima.

The Gran Sabana is an upland plateau of coarse grassland interspersed with areas of woodland. that extends from Surinam west to the Sierra Macarena in Colombia and from the Orinoco in the north to the Rio Branco in Brazil to the south. The most notable feature of the region are the 2-3,000 metre table mountains known as tepuy.

Ilu Tepuy

At first, we didn't think of the mountain in a proprietary way. We were looking for a mountain, any mountain really, that had not been climbed and Ilu–Tepuy seemed to offer the best possibilities since there was a 'path' to its base. This didn't mean there was a path in our sense of the word necessarily, but that someone has been there and, knowing this, people would be prepared to go there again without too much difficulty.

We knew about the Tepuy from Douglas Branch, an Englishman resident in Caracas. He had been to the mountain twice. Ilu Tepuy is the first noticeable mountain in the Roriama chain. Although I had been to the Gran Sabana on three other occasions, this was the first time I had seen the mountain clearly. It has the classic table-mountain form but is much smaller than Roraima.

The top was much smaller than we expected and almost flat with little vegetation and smooth black slabs with deep crevasses to carry the main crater over the vertical sides. We stayed an hour taking photographs, then raced back to the camp to get there before dark.

Later, on a visit to the botanic garden in Caracas we found references to Ilu Tepuy in Julian Steyemark's book, Contribuciones a la Flora de Venezuela. There were at least two previous expeditions to Kerauren and Ilu Tepuy prior

Panorama of the Gran Sabana looking north. Left to right: Ilu Tepuy, Karaurin, Wadakapiapué, Yuruanai Tepuy, Kukenan and Roriama. Perai Tepuy in the foreground

Panorama of the Gran Sabana looking north east. Left to right: Ilu Tepuy, Wadakapiapué, Kukenan and Roriama.

to Douglas Branch's two expeditions. These were by Phelps and Steyermark, from the botanic garden Caracas, in October-December 1944 and Maguire and Wurdach, from the botanic garden, New York, in December 1952. Both these expeditions were botanical. They reached the col between Ilu Tepuy and Kukenan where they pitched their base camp and did not attempt to climb the tepuy.

Caracas, Quebrada de los Chorros

We had spent a couple of weeks in Caracas visiting firned and planning what to do and we needed some exercise so we decided to spend a day descending a quebra

Quebradas are steep gorges with waterfalls that cut through the forest and dense vegetation of the mountain-sides. They can be very long, dropping over 6,000 feet and taking a couple of days to descend. They are exciting, take you to isolated places where no one has been before and are a cool escape from the baking weather of the dry season in the city.

Steve lived in Venezuela from 1970-1975 and from his flat in Chuao there was a superb panorama of the coastal range. Almost directly opposite there was a huge quebrada that snaked down the whole of the Avila from the ridge between Pico Oriental and Pico Naiguata, the two highest points on the mountain chain. If you looked closely you could see a tall waterfall on an s-shaped bend about two-thirds of the way down from the top. After two

Scharlie, beginning of descent

First abseil

failed attempts, when he had had to climb the vertical rock wall to escape, he finally managed to descend it with David Nott's son, Vivien. He repeated the trip several times, including once with his son Jonathan who was only nine at the time, and had even made a film of the descent with Daniel and Wilmur that had taken three days, sleeping in hammocks to the early morning sounds of howler monkeys.

Monday 19/10/81 Quebrada los Chorros, Caracas
We got up in the dark and packed the rucksacks with two extra long ropes Daniel had lent us, an orange each and my camera in a tupperware container. It was a grey morning but the autopista was almost clear of traffic as we drove to the Avila. For breakfast we bought an arepa with ham and two café con leche at a roadside caravan, then drove further up the Cota Mil to a car park above Sebucan where we began the a steep climb to Paraiso. Here we could start the decent of the Quebrada Los Choros, or Tocome as it is named on some maps.

We had been glad of the mist as we climbed but wished the sun would come out as we waded downstream. We were wearing shoes, jeans and long-

The big abseil

Nearing the end

sleeved shirts to protect us from scratches, but although glossy large-leaves tropical plants grew thickly on the banks, there were surprisingly few thorns or tangled undergrowth. It felt as if someone must have cleared the way. Steve says he has seen snakes sun-bathing on rocks here, but today there was no sun and we saw nothing but butterflies – several of the large shimmering blue ones moving like bats among the trees. There was more water than Steve had seen before.

The rocks were round and smooth and we sat and slid down them, especially in one place where there was a chute about fifteen feet long. We shot down it and sank into the deep pool at the bottom, bobbed up again and swam to shallow water, our rucksacks inflating with air on our backs. After a long while, we came to the first big fall that plunged over the rocks more than 150 ft. The sun came out for a few dazzling minutes and we took off our clothes and basked in it.

The sun didn't last long. Soon, big, cold drops of rain came swishing down. Wet clothes were warmer than none, so we dressed quickly and set about abseiling down the falls from a tree. We had to avoid the main fall, as the pressure of water was so great.

Too cold to stop and rest, on and on, shivering, saturated, but exhilarated we plunged on down, scrambling up the slippery banks where the river was too full, sliding down great fallen trees and using the ropes again and again. We neared the bottom of the gorge, and knew it must be evening, because the tree frogs had started to croak.

People in the bread shop let Steve move to the front of the queue as he

El Avila with Ramon Blanco

Asleep in the shade

was soaking wet from head to toe. Ice cold beer and hot bread rolls in the jeep and home to Wilmur and his family in Cumbres de Curumo. (Wilmur was a friend from when Steve lived in Caracas in the seventies.)

Tuesday 20/10/81 Dia del Censo, Los Teques
The government has decreed that everyone must stay at home for the day to be censored or risk being imprisoned or shot. We spent the day quietly with Chino at Los Teques. No fewer than four census officials visited us. How on earth will they manage in the rancho areas if they spend this much time on the three houses on this one little road.

Gran Sabana

Monday 26/10/81
Today we tried to organise transport to La Gran Sabana. The aeroplane to Ciudad Bolivar leaves at 6 pm. but we are told that all the onward flights to Santa Elena are full. However, there is no way to book a seat except by flying to Ciudad Bolivar. Have all the passengers been waiting there for days? Is it gold rush fever? We hear that gold has been discovered recently and that there is a food shortage in Santa Elena.

There is no bus all the way to the Gran Sabana, but once a day a coach leaves for Tumeremo, a small town on the way, and arrives at nine in the

Dia del Censo with Chino and friend

Scharlie in El Dorado

morning. The cost is a third of the airfare and we are told we will have no problem getting a jeep from there. We tried to calculate how much food we will need for perhaps four weeks and go to a supermarket to buy dried soup, rice, porridge, sugar and dried milk.

Wednesday 28/10/81
Nuevo Circo, the bus station near the old centre of Caracas,. The buses are moving at walking pace, so we walk hot and heavy. Inside it is a cattle market with us going to the highest bidder. We find our way to the ticket office through a frenzy of hands and voices and only just avoid being carried off to the wrong bus. The drivers pay these men to find customers. Our bus is an Autobus Expresos del Oriente coach that leaves for Ciudad Bolivar at 6:30 in the evening.

We are first on the bus, but the front seat is 'occupado' the driver says. A fat pasty looking boy walks down the bus leaving cards on everyone's laps. The card announces that he is dumb and politely requests 1 Bolivar. He walks back, collecting his cards and his money. He has more success than the men selling jewellery, plastic toys, or fruit. Then a man selling trays decorated with exotic Chinese prints comes on board and does a roaring trade.

All this time, the engine has been running. Petrol makes this country rich, but the traffic in Caracas will soon come to a standstill. The cars move endlessly nose to tail on the autopista. Hawkers weave their way amongst them selling fruit and newspapers.

Señor Buckley

The prospector and his jeep

The bus is comfortable and we drive all night, stopping twice for refreshment and a loo break. Scharlie sleeps deeply and does not notice when we cross the Orinoco at dawn. We pass though Upata, Guasipati, El Callao and arrive in Tumeremo more or less on time. This is the end of the line for our bus and we start hitching.

Thursday 29/10/81 Kilometer 88
We arrive in El Dorado, with its small asphalted square, bar and a general store. The jungle has been cleared since Raleigh came this way in search for gold but there is still mining that the government tries to discourage because it pollutes the rivers and destroys the forest.

We cadge a lift for 50 Bolivars from a Señor Vargas, a friendly fat man with a truck-load of children and a tortoise that I rescue from under the accelerator pedal. We reach Kilometer 88 at midday and find a place for lunch of spaghetti and beans or chicken and rice while we wait for a lift. Lots of lorries pass at Christmas and Easter, they tell us, but not today. Señor Vargas says there is a goldmine here that is one hundred and forty years old. Recently more gold has been discovered and lots of people are coming to try their luck. We are stuck and have to find a place to sleep. We end up on a concrete floor in the miners' quarters.

Kamoirán rapids km 771

Kama Meru km 820 with Ramon Blanco

Friday 30/10/81, Kama Meru

We rise at dawn and get a lift with an agronomist in his blue Toyota jeep. He is here on holiday and trying his hand at prospecting. There is a gleaming pick, shovel and panning dish in the back of the jeep. In winding curves, the dirt road climbs over a thousand metres from the flood plain of the Orinoco up to the plateau grassland of the Gran Sabana. It steepens at the Piedra de la Virgen, a huge black rock by the right side of the road and continues up La Escalera to top out at the Soldado Pionero, the monument to the military engineers who built the road in the early seventies. The road to the Apongua Falls and the mission at Kavanayen we visited with the children the second Christmas we were in Venezuela in 1971, dives off to the right just here.

We stop to bathe in the river near some beautiful rapids. From here we can see the first mountains in the range of tepuys running south to Roraima.

We drive on to the Kama Meru Falls where there is settlement of a couple of houses and a round open-sided thatched shelter for travellers next to the river.

It is mid-day and we say good-bye to the prospector. We meet two locals, Ramon Blanco and Cecilio Vasquez. They confirm that the pretty mountain we were looking at further up the road is Ilu Tepuy, the mountain we have come to climb.

Douglas Branch, an Englishman resident in Caracas, had told us about Ilu Tepuy. He had tried and failed to climb it twice. Although I had been to the Gran Sabana three times, this was the first time I had seen the mountain

Our first meal with our shiny pan

Kama Meru Falls

Sunset on the brink of the falls

clearly. Ilu Tepuy has the classic table-mountain shape but, although the same height, is much smaller than Roraima and looks rather like a funnel atop a green ship.

We arrange with Ramon Blanco to guide us, starting out the following day, and agree a price of 50 Bs (about £5) a day.

We explore the river, walking over water worn slabs to the brink of the waterfall and then clamber down to get a photo looking back at the falls. Back in the shelter we get out the spanking new saucepan we bought in Caracas and collect wood and make our supper, the first of many we'll cook over an open fire. The sand flies are unbelievably bad in the night, sleeping in the open next to the water. They feel like spiders' webs settling on one's face.

The Gran Sabana is an upland plateau of coarse grassland interspersed

Crossing River Kama

A delightful dip

with areas of woodland. It is part of a region known as the Guyanan Shield that extends from the Talfenberg in Surinam west to the Sierra Macarena in Colombia and from the Orinoco in the north to the Rio Branco in Brazil to the south. The most notable feature of the region are the 2-3,000 metre table mountains of the Roraima series known as tepuy in Pemon, the language of the Taurepane, who live in this area, and as jidi in Yekuana the language of the Makiritare who Steve visited various times on tributaries of the Orinoco further west.

Much of Indian mythology involves stories about these mountains. The remnants of the Caledonian seabed eroded differentially to form these sandstone mesas and buttes – table mountains that are flat-topped and have vertical or overhanging walls rising to a maximum height of 9,000 feet. The two most famous are Roraima, featured in the Lost World of Conan Doyle, and the Auyan-Tepuy, from which Angel Falls, the highest waterfall in the world, tumbles. The rock is generally hard, being of a similar consistency to millstone, or it would not have resisted the erosion of millions of years.

Saturday, 31/10/81, Uroy Uaray to Unonori Pa
It turns out that Ramon Blanco can't take us after all as he's going diamond hunting. So we walk four kilometres along the blinding hot dusty road to another group of houses called Uroy Uaray.

Crossing the sabana

About twenty people come out to meet us and say we must be mad to want to climb a mountain. Nevertheless, two young men, Jose Luis Martinez and Ramiro Pascon, agree to come and we set off almost at once. Jose Luis takes the lead, and Ramiro Pascon, who does not seem too bright, carries the big red bag with the ropes and what little climbing gear we've brought. He's so tiny the bag almost touches the ground. We have light rucksacks, but they offer to carry Scharlie's so she is fancy free.

It's hot, but when we come to a river we plunge in fully clothed and dry out as we walk. The cooling sensation as the moisture evaporates is delightful. We walk all day across a wide grassy plain. Frequently we wade through rivers waist deep and see occasional palm trees in boggy ground glowing a lurid green.

Finally, we pass through woods and a cultivated clearing to a communal house or maloca called Unonori Pa. The twenty people living here seem to be related to Jose Luis. We are offered casava bread and pink, slightly alcoholic, cachire. We stop and rest whilst Jose Luis catches up on the news.

One of the women is baking casaba or cassava bread – the flat white cakes that are the staple food of the Taurepan. She piles the coarse flour in the centre of a sheet of iron supported on four stout sticks over a wood fire. She

Washing in a stream

spreads the flour with a circular motion of her hands until it lays in a round half inch layer about two feet wide. She leaves it to bake for five minutes, occasionally smoothing the surface or stoking the fire. Then she slips a woven mat under the cake and deftly turns it over to bake on the other side. Before beginning to brown, she slips the cake off the griddle onto an adjacent table to cool and begins the process again, scooping the flour from a dugout log to one side of the fire.

When cool, the floppy cakes are removed from the table and laid on leaves in the grass to dry in the sun. Fresh, the bread is soft and can be folded. After a day or two the cakes harden and become brittle but remain edible for a long time. They last Feliciano's family two weeks and provide an excellent food for a hunting people on the move a lot of the time.

The mosquitoes are bad here and we move on to a pleasant camp by fast moving water where there are relatively few. It is dark by the time we have eaten. Tonight we decide to put up the tent, which is just as well as it rains. Jose Luis built a palm shelter and got a fire going in spite of the damp. We had a good night's sleep and were up at dawn.

Sunday, 1/11/81, Unonori Pa to Uarpa
Over breakfast, Cecilio Acosta, an older man who everyone seems to respect, announces that he's coming with us. It seems to be decided so we don't argue or ask why. He seems to be a shaman.

We repack the sacks, and the Indians take enough food for two days, which implies they don't think we'll last long. They fold the still soft cassava wheels

Lunch break of raisins and sandflies

The indians used fire to manage the land

into their woven panniers. This with a bottle of chille sauce is all the food they take, although they carry a shotgun and obviously hope to hunt something.

We walk all day through woods and across open grassland to within sight of the rock summit. We see a giant anteater galloping out of sight into a patch of trees, luckily before the Indians can get off a shot. We pass a high rock with a distinctive white mark in the shape of a heron, that gives its name to the maloca.

The path gives out so we cut a path towards the base of the wall. It has been raining hard for some days and the rock is wet and slippery. Steve gets out the ropes, puts on his rock boots and and tries climbing. But it all seems very hard and he does not get that far before having to come back down. There is no obvious line up the first rock band that is about two hundred feet high. Although we can't see it because we are right underneath the wall, we know that above the rock band there is a band of vegetation and a way to the massive chimney line we could see from far away. So if we can only climb this cliff we stand a good chance of getting to the top. We decide to try again tomorrow.

We make camp. There is no running water although everywhere is dripping and we are wet and cold. The mosquitoes and sand flies are terrible. Then disaster strikes. Steve eye is inflamed and he takes out his contact lens to rest his eye. But it slips out of his cold fingers and drops into a crack in the rocks and is lost. Luckily he has a spare. Scharlie has left her Lillets behind and her period has started. What to do? Moss?

We feel miserable, but the Indians are relaxed, kind and cheerful as always.

Cecilio crossing the sabana

Drying out after a wet night

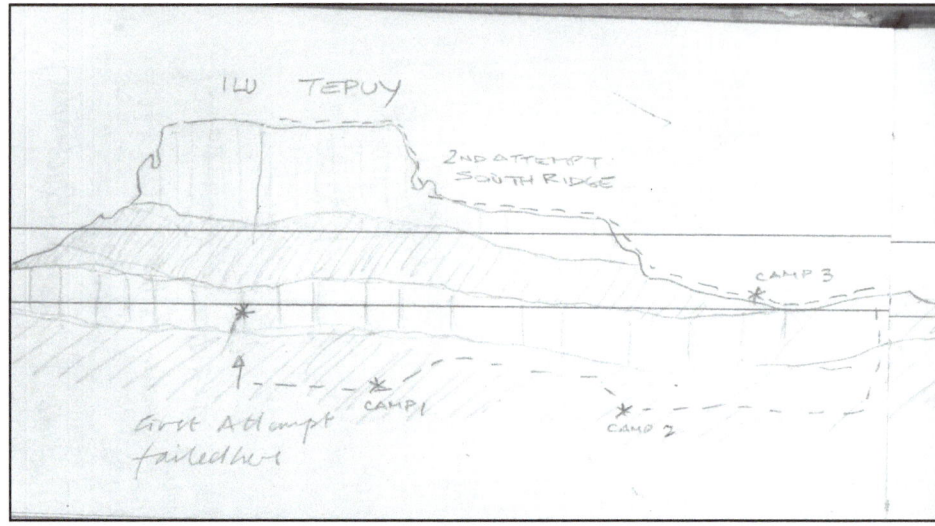

So we get out the tent and pitch it in the best place we can find, which is not ideal because the ground is so uneven and rocky. The Indians make a fire and we share our food. The plaga of sandflies and mosquitoes abate and we sit around the fire chatting.

2/11/81 Monday, Uarpa
The rocks are hard to lie on without a camper mat and there is a thunderstorm that lasts for over an hour. The tent pole at our feet collapses because we have been unable to pitch the tent properly and we are soaked from the knees

Uonori-pa with Feliciano Gonzalez

Rest break, team pensive

down. We can hear the Indians gently grumbling outside and they ask if we have waterproof coats. We have only the clothes we stand up in plus fleece jackets to keep us warm at night. We lend them these, which is all we have. Despite everything we have a surprisingly good night and wake refreshed.

The Indians look amazingly dry in the morning. Cecilio holds the box of matches towards the fire to dry them off. Without much discussion we decide to retreat as the rock was now pouring with run-off and the alternative route of cutting a path to the col between Ilu Tepuy and Kerauren would take another two or three days.

Back at the maloca we meet Feliciano Gonzalez, a handsome young man

Cecilio's children

Ilu Tepuy

they call Capitan who seems to be headman of the village. They give us a little woven basket and a cassava cake to take away and tell us ever so politely that we should bring presents next time we come. Walking onwards in the evening is perfect. There are no mosquitoes, and it is cool and bright. The mountains very beautiful and Steve makes a sketch. We camp in the woods with Feliciano and his family who have caught us up and now share their meal of cassava, baked fish and spinach. We lie on the bare earth in the leaf litter under the trees and go to sleep.

Tuesday, 3/11/81, La Laja
Leaving Jose Luis and the others we have a long hot walk back across the savannah to the road that we reach by late morning. We spend the afternoon bathing and washing our clothes then waiting for them to dry. In the evening we get a lift to La Laja, a few kilometres up the road towards Santa Elena. We have decided to climb Roraima. It was the obvious thing to do, Steve hadn't done it before and we knew we would get up it and achieve something.

Wednesday 4/11/81, La Laja
We spend a comfortable night and lazy day sunbathing and swimming. It is a beautiful spot and it is great to have a rest day as there is virtually no plaga (insects). There are no fish in the river either and the water leaves a filmy white

Typical patches of forest in the sabana

Scharlie taller than Jose Luis and Ramiro

deposit on the skin. We try to get a lift in the evening but the only one going our way is full. So we resign ourselves to stopping another night and make a meal with the last remnants of our food.

Thursday 5/11/81, Santa Elena

We wake at dawn to the sound of heavy vehicles passing. I poke my head out of the tent and see three huge timber lorries grinding their way across the ford in the river. I think of running to stop them since they are going quite slowly, but it will take us a while to get packed and they won't want to wait for us. We get up straight away and dress but it's a waste of time since there are no more vehicles until after lunch. When will we learn?

We make a fire, cook and eat our porridge, pack and then laze around in the river all the rest of the day waiting for a lift. We finally get one at two in the afternoon with an empty timber lorry that is returning to Brazil. The huge lorry drove into the ford on the water worn rocks where we were lounging in the water. The driver and a couple of soldiers look down from the cab and decide to join us. They all get in and have a bath – one doing press-ups covered in soap.

They give us a bone shaking, break-neck lift with us sitting on the empty bed of the lorry. We sit right behind the cab but we are still in a cloud of dust and Steve is in misery with grit in his eyes. We pay for the driver's meal when we stop at a road side lean-to.

Finally we reach Santa Elena at about three and are stopped at the cabala, a sort of customs post. An officious, grinning soldier tells us to stand on one side

Ilu Tepuy in cloud

Botanising – irises

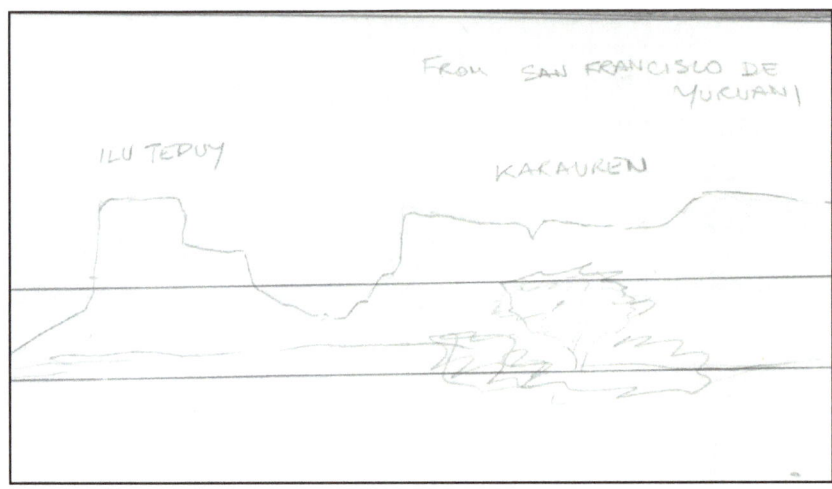

of the road. Another says we can sit in the square. Scharlie is upset because her towel got left by the river where we were swimming.

We go off exploring. Santa Elena itself has grown, as one would expect, given the mining boom and tourism. The plaza is well treed and there are now four or five restaurants and an ice-cream parlour. The Italian restaurateur that Steve met when he came here in 1972 has gone back to Italy. Surprisingly, there are none of the bars one might have expected in a frontier mining town. Maybe Icabaru is the fleshpot now.

The mission is just as it was, clean, cool and polished. But Padre Diego has returned to Spain and Padre Tirso has moved to Kavanayen. The clearing where Padre Tirso picked grapefruits for the children eight years ago is now

Brief rest in the shade

Botanising – orchids

a neat orchard with fat cattle. The Indian village is beautiful with clean, paved streets and well-ordered houses.

When we arrive, they are slaughtering a calf. We can hear the thud of the axe but do not go and look. I remember how distressed the children had been to see a cow being slaughtered when we came here ten years ago.

We stuff ourselves with bananas, fresh bread, buns and a hot meal, then find a store to buy supplies. We try to get a lift back to San Francisco de Yuruani, where the path to Roraima starts, but no one is going our way. We meet a man in the restaurant who promises us a lift in the morning. He is leaving at 5am and says that he will wake us. We pitch the tent on a grassy patch near the entrance to the town so we'll be ready. It is a bit like sleeping on a traffic island. The plaga is bad so we have to sleep with the tent zipped up and so pass a hot and airless night.

Roraima

Friday 6/11/81, Perai Tepuy
We get up in the dark, determined not to be late again, and sit on a wall wrapped in a sleeping bag waiting for the jeep driver. He turns up well after dawn and apologises that he won't be able take us because his car is full. But we are offered a lift in lorry soon after for 40 Bs.

In the restaurant we heard a woman talking to her children in English. It turns out that her name is Mrs. Buckley and that her husband had an Australian

Perai Tepuy, en route to Roraima

Perai Tepuy

Scharlie with Roraima (right) and Kukenan (left)

grandfather. She, her husband and children all speak English although they look Indian. They warmly invite us to their home and say we can leave the ropes and climbing gear there as we don't need them to climb Roraima.

We leave about ten. From San Francisco de Yuruani where the lift drops us, we walk an obvious track to the village of Perai Tepuy. This is where Ambrosio Perez lives, the Indian guide who came to Kukunan Tepui when Steve climbed it with Ramon and Hans in 1972.

It is hot. The yhenny (sandflies) buzz round our eyes providing us with the

Ascent ramp above Scharlie's right sholder

Looking back down the ramp

impetus to steam up the long hot hill, hoping it will improve at the top in the wind. They are still there at the top and with us nearly all day long except for a lunchtime respite when we swim in a stream. They don't seem to obey any law of temperature or time of day. We reach Parai Tepuy about 6 p.m. and are offered the schoolhouse to sleep in. The people here are much less friendly and do not offer us anything to eat or drink. They are obviously fed up with back-packing visitors. Carlos, younger brother of Ambrosio, now lives in new house at bottom of the hill surrounded by a wire fence with fruit bushes.

Saturday, 7/11/81, en route to Roraima
It has been difficult to get clear directions to Roraima and we make several false starts. Distances are foreshortened, valleys disappear and you can easily set off along a ridge in entirely the wrong direction. It turns out that we should have climbed up from the village and walked round in a great loop on the high plateau but we descend to the quebrada and have a long hot climb up again.

Two hours' walking brings a green tent into view and two tall blond

East along the cliff face

Waterworn slab

Germans, Emil and Kim, eating a leisurely breakfast. One has climbed Roraima before and is taking his friend and plans to spend several days on top. They are carrying at least 60 lbs. each, so are walking very slowly. They give us clear directions to a 'base camp' at the foot of the rock wall and to the cave on the summit. An Indian in the village also mentioned this cave.

The path goes on for mile after mile across the grassy dry savannah, all colour washed out in the mid-day sun. At times we choose different paths, walking on parallel tracks up to a half-mile apart. This is a source of some friction. Steve, having been in the area before goes ahead, but Scharlie wants to go her own way and where the paths diverged she invariably chooses a different way.

We stop at the second big river we have to wade across and rest under a tree, lunching on Toddy, a Venezuela powdered milk chocolate drink, and dates. The Germans arrive as we are about to leave.

The next four hours are punishing walking uphill in burning heat and meeting erratic clouds of yhenny. Roraima and Kukenan rear up impressively in front of us. They seem close but we do not reach 'base camp' till 4 pm, feeling footsore and weary. We collect water and make a fire. The Germans loom out of the dark and say we are five minutes short of the true base camp. But the place we have chosen is clean, untrammelled and nearer the water.

Roraima summit formation

Sunday, 8/11/81, Roraima

We climb up through forest and along a spur to the bottom of the ramp rising like a staircase from right to left across the face of the mountain. This was the route of the first ascent by im Thurm in 1884. Interestingly im Thurm went on to become a government agent in British Guiana and was employed on the Venezuelan boundary commission of 1897-99 that carved off a huge chunk of Venezuela, that is still in dispute and hatched on Venezuelan maps as the Zona en Reclamación.

There is a good river here and a camp could be made here to allow an attempt on a direct route up Roraima. The normal way goes left, climbing up the forested ramp, with a small descent round a bluff at half-height.

The ramp takes us about three hours. We are in humid mist most of the way so cannot see the view and just glimpse the rock wall rising 2,000 ft. above us. We arrive at the top about 2 pm. We have no watch and guess the time by the sun and don't feel its lack. We follow a path rightwards to an overhanging rock that is known as the cave-camp. We feel weak and have little energy. We have been living on porridge, sugar and powdered milk for breakfast, two or three dates for lunch and rice and packet soup at night with tea and toddy for extras. Clearly, given how hard we are working, this is not enough. Nevertheless, after pitching the tent and making a fire to dry wood placed above it, we walk north-west towards the trig. point that marks the three way frontier with Guyana and Brazil.

Pictures have prepared us for the summit of Roraima. im Thurm did not find live prehistoric monsters there, but there are fantastic creatures of stone

Roraima summit

as well as turreted castles and giant mushrooms. Strange vegetation grows in the round pools of still water. The summit of Roraima is a labyrinth and you can lose yourself in minutes. In the early morning and the evening the slanting light brings the place alive and strangely beautiful. In the strong mid-day sun it becomes arid and almost monotonous.

It is six hours walk to the trig. point. We find the river of crystal and a deep lake at the bottom of a round crater.

We spend the night in the cave in brilliant moonlight and blessedly with no mosquitoes. We are going to sleep soon after dark at 8 pm and waking at 5 am with the light.

Monday 9/11/81, Roraima
The night is cold and we get a night's rest. We would have loved to stay here several days but have only brought enough food for one day. We walk back to ascent route and leave our sacks and go off to explore. We try to walk to the cliff edge facing Kukenan but walking is not easy as the rock plateau has been scored by rivers that have formed deep gullies. It takes us two or three hours to climb down into these gullies and up the cliffs on the opposite side. We cross three to within sight of whole of Kukenan, but the mountain is in cloud and we turn back to the ramp. The waterfalls are now much bigger and the descent is slippy.

View of Kukenan from Roraima

Scharlie finds a huge quartz crystal formation on matrix of sandstone. It weighs a couple of kilos and somebody must have broken it off in the river of crystal and then, when it got too heavy to carry, must have dropped it on the path. Scharlie wants to take it back. I say you must be joking, then slip it into my pack when she has gone ahead. We wade across the Kukenan River and then the Camaguata and reach the base camp about six.

Tuesday 10/11/81, Perai Tepuy
We get up early and leave at first light after a breakfast of cold rice pudding and raisins. After a long tiring walk reach Perai Tepuy at 7am. Ambrosio is still away so do not stop.

We take a pica or path on way back, instead of road. The path crosses two streams, the first of which is larger and good to bathe in. We strip off and marvel at how thin we both are. We make Toddy, a life-saver on a long, hot, yhenny filled walk. Scharlie's hair, stiff with soap, dries instantly.

Just after midday, at a point near a clump of trees growing on a rock mound, where two jeep tracks diverge, we meet Señor Buckley and the Commissario from San Francisco coming to pick up a sick man with fever from Perai Tepuy.

It takes another two and a half hours to reach San Francisco, where we find a meal and wait for a lift. We return to Santa Elena to pick up the gear we have left spend the night at Señor Buckley's.

Bathing in the river

Wednesday 11/11/81, Tumeremo

We are up early but have trouble persuading lorries to take us. Eventually one of a group of lorries agrees to take us. The driver is called Antonio. He is Brazilian and, like all the other lorries, he is carting huge thick fresh cut baulks of mahogany. We climb into the cab. It is primitive hot and noisy grinding along in low gear. Scharlie is perched on the gearbox cover and every time Steve drops off to sleep, Antonio makes advances. We stop to bathe at a waterfall and by midday we are still two hours from Km 88 when the lorry breaks down. Antonio says there is some trouble with the gearbox and we have to wait while it cools.

We have a meal with the drivers at the Portuguese truck stop. It is twice as expensive as Señor Vargas' restaurant in Tumeremo. The woman is rude and mean and charges us 8Bs each for badly made coffee and stale bread. But her animals, three dogs and some deer in an enclosure in the garden, are unusually well cared for.

The truck still refuses to move so we persuade two other drivers to take us but they insist we have to travel separately. I am highly suspicious. It is six hours to Tumeremo and a great trial for Scharlie as she has to spend the entire time resisting the ardour of her driver, Jino who was trying to teach her Portuguese with a limited vocabulary of words like kiss.

I have to keep telling my driver to stop and wait to let her lorry catch up and after an hour or so insist she swop lorries and so we can travel together. It turns out that they do not believe we are married because she is not wearing a ring.

Centre of Choroni

Colonial house where we slung hammocks

Finally we reach Tumeremo at 2am in the morning and sleep on the wooden planks on the lorry trailer. It feels remarkable soft and comfortable after the rock we having been lying on, but in the morning we are covered in red dust.

Thursday 12/11/81, Tumeremo
In the morning we have café con leche and huevos revueltos, scrambled egg with onion and peppers, in Señor Vargas' Italian Restaurant. We sit killing time in the square since the bus does not leave till late afternoon. Two lads come over to start trouble but I tell them that I have always found Venezuelans to be as polite and well mannered as the English. They relax and suddenly start being friendly. They say that they thought we were Americans.

To pass the time we saunter down the main street and find a café. Three men and some women are talking in loud voices, never looking around except to order another beer or to leer when a curvy girl walks past in the street. Then we are harassed for hour or so by a red-eyed tipsy young man and his equally drunken friend, a policeman, who want us to stay the night at his house.

We are highly relieved to board the bus. The driver plays loud salsa music and people chat loudly all night and we keep stopping at offices and cafés but we must have slept because we reach Caracas at dawn and don't feel we had been travelling that long. Crossing the Orinoco in the dark was magnificent with the lights of the dam and the hydroelectric plant and the glow from the Siderurgica Nacional – a new steel city bursting with energy.

Beach Choroni

All to ourselves

Friday 13/11/81, Caracas

Caracas bus station at dawn is as busy as mid-day, but thankfully much cooler. The taxi driver asks 50 Bs to take us to Wilmer's but we catch a bus instead for only 5 Bs.

We shower and feed, and then we try to organise a weekend at the beach. Gonzales will lend us his house in Choroni, but we have no car. We ring Daniel to tell him how we have got on and to say we plan to go back to Ilu Tepuy and want to invite Douglas if he will come. Despite the complete failure of our first attempt I am confident that we can climb it and since he has tried to climb it twice it seems fair to offer him the chance to come. We invite Daniel to come with us, but he is in love with a ballet dancer who lives in New York where he visited a mystic who had told him to chill for three months and not do anything.

We borrow a jeep from Daniel and drive to Choroni for a well-earned rest at the beach. Choroni is one of Steve's favourite places and still unspoilt. There is a switch back dirt road across the mountains. Nevertheless, the intelligensia of Caracas have 'discovered' it and have renovated many of the colonial style houses.

On Monday we drive up into the hills southeast of Caracas along dirt roads to a small farm. Douglas is tall and thin with a beard and earns his living

Scenes from Choroni

furniture making. He is friendly and helpful but despite my encouragement does not want to come with us – he has something arranged and cannot change his plans. I try to explain that I think we'll climb it but I don't think he quite believes us. He's been there before after all and maybe my confidence is misplaced.

We spend the afternoon going to a supermarket to buy food for the trip and packing. It's very simple – our staples are tea bags, porridge, milk powder and papellon or dark brown cane sugar in a block for breakfast, raisins and boiled sweets for lunch and to give children, and for dinner, rice or pasta plus packet soup for flavouring plus sardines or canned meat as a treat. This keeps you alive but you lose a lot of weight on this kind of diet. On the other hand you have to carry the stuff.

Our gear was equally basic. Since we had no car, and travelled by bus or hitch-hiked we travelled as light as possible, carrying (apart from ropes which José Luis carried) all the gear and food for two weeks packed in small rucksacks with outside pockets. This desire to travel light, governed most of our decisions. Firstly, how to camp. Ideally one would, in the lowest camps, sleep in hammocks with mosquito nets under a communal tarpaulin and have a tent for the high camp above the tree line. Since it rained most nights and it was imperative to sleep warm and dry before making an attempt on the upper

wall, we decided to take a very light two-man tent called a Saunders GC2 that weighed less than 2 kilos and to dispense with the luxury of hammocks in the lower camps. This plan worked but it would have been better to have taken light hammocks since one of the Indians could have carried the extra load without difficulty. Scharlie's hollowfill sleeping bag dried much quicker than my old down bag, but was bulkier. We had fitted long zips to both which meant we could unzip when it was hot.

We took only the clothes we stood in, jeans and long sleeved cotton shirts, plus polar jackets for the cooler nights. Since we could wash in streams and dry out quickly in the sun we didn't miss having a change, except returning on the bus. However, an old pair of silk pyjamas to change into at night would have been lovely. For footwear, we went for maximum comfort since we had so far to walk. We walked three or four hundred miles in the five weeks we spent in the Gran Sabana. Scharlie chose trainers and I used Spanish Fell boots with canvas uppers. Both were fine. As regards climbing gear, we took two 50m long 9 mm ropes, PA rock boots, five nuts, and four tapes.

Scharlie with her parakeet present

Learning to use a cerbatana (blowpipe)

Yuca or Cassava (Manihot esculenta)

Yuca root

Grated then boiled to extract poison

Squashed in woven sebucan

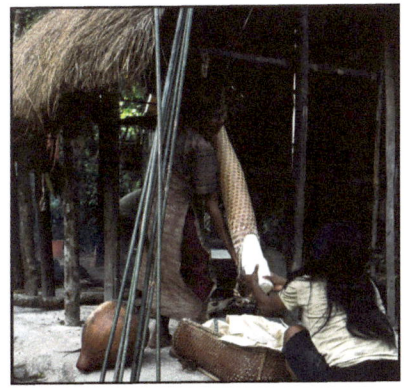
Poison extracted

Sieving flour

Ilu Tepuy

Tuesday 17/11/81, Tumeremo
We catch the early morning bus from Nuevo Circo to Tumeremo again and journey to the Gran Sabana in record time. Although we leave the Caracas bus station an hour late we arrive an hour and a half earlier than the first time.

Wednesday 18/11/81, Uroy Uray to Uarpa
At Tumeremo, we discover that there is a Toyota transport to Santa Elena. At 9.30 am thirteen people and luggage board – the driver and his two friends, three Brazilians returning home, a Venezuelan soldier going back to

Casaba cake

Drying in the sun

Sampling the fish stew

A present of peppers in a wicker basket

his barracks in Sta Elena, four Indians and us. Despite colliding with a 'panfi', a black curassow the size of a turkey that flew up startled and cracked our windscreen and the driver hopped out and collected it for dinner, we make it to Uroy Uruay in the early afternoon compared with the lorry that took eleven hours.

When we arrived the village was being vaccinated. We go straight to Jose Luis' home and he came out to greet us. He said he would come with us tomorrow. His family – wife, his three boys, José Luis Eduardo, Luciano and Angel, and cousin – shared their meal of cassava and fish with us. We present a new pair of boots to Jose Luis and presents for the children we bought in Caracas. We are going to sleep on the floor in the thatched hut next to them. Steve made a fire and José Luis immediately chopped some wood and brought it to us. They were so courteous. Ramon Blanco has just turned up with an axe over his shoulder and a bag full of batteries, etc.

We heard singing and went along to the schoolhouse where an Adventist meeting had started – hymns and testimonies and a Bible story given by the teacher all in Pemon. We are invited to the service by Franco, the village school teacher.

We feel better after a rest with food inside us. We return to go to bed only to find that we had left the lid of the powered milk unscrewed and the dog had run off with all our milk powder. Stumbling around in the dark, all we could find was the lid and a bit of spilt powder. It felt like a major catastrophe and we had a row about it. Trivial things take on a huge importance when you are in extreme situations.

Fish stew, pepers, sweet potato and cachire

Cecilio fooling around

Thursday 19/11/81, Uroy Uroay

In the morning we tell the family about the mishap and everyone scatters to look for the canister but without success. Later, the dog turns up with white powder on his nose. Everyone is amused and we join in the laughter. The search was renewed and the half empty canister found. We were able to buy a new tin from the schoolmaster and made a present of the remainder to the dog.

We divided the load into three and set off with José Luis. Scharlie usually finds it difficult to walk over the same ground, but it's pleasant and we reached Uarpa, where Cecilio lives, by midday. All the village are gathered for a meal and we are treated royally. No-one wants to go anywhere today and Steve goes off to clear the forest for a new canuco with all the men. They work a

About to set off, Ilu Tepui in background

Jose Luis

while, clearing brush, then return. Where the foliage had died they cleared the larger trees.

The men showed us the canes they cut for weaving and how to peel the pith away. It is men's work and every man can weave. Now they make baskets for sale as well as their own use.

A little boy brought in a parrot he had winged with his blowpipe. His mother offered it to Scharlie as a present when she saw she liked it and was a little put out when Scharlie regretfully refused. Blowpipes come in different

The base of the wall

Cutting a traverse below the wall

sizes – the largest we saw was about eight feet long. A cane dart with cotton wrapped round one end is inserted into the mouthpiece end and blown up the tube with great accuracy and force.

The women were working till after dark, making casava for the men to take with them. Feliciano's sister-in-law was bent over a dug out log rubbing the white tubers of the freshly cut and peeled yuca on a flat board, like an old fashioned washboard, but studded with small, sharp stones. The tuber was shredded into a fine stringy mass in the bottom of the log. This was then taken and loaded into a woven tube about 7' long and 6" diameter. This tube, called a sebucan, has a loop at both ends and is suspended from a stout forked pole embedded in the ground. A pole is inserted in the bottom loop and by pressing down the venomous juice of the yuca is extracted into a vessel below. As more juice is extracted and the wet flour compressed by the narrowing and lengthening tube, the lever pole is moved down a notch in a second pole inserted vertically in the ground about four to five feet away. After leaving the tube to drain, the mass, now compressed into cylindrical shapes is returned to the dug out log. Finally the women rub the flour through a coarse sieve.

On our travels, we saw various refinements to this process. In San Francisco de Yuruani there was also a clay oven, known as a ptari, that concentrated the fire below a circular iron plate. We also saw a mechanical grater made from a milk tin. Holes had been punched into it so it resembled a cheese grater and the metal had been mounted on a short round log. This was then rolled backwards and forwards over the yuca in a wooden box and the coarse shreds fell through a slit out in the bottom. It didn't look very well used and

Cecilio climbs a tree to spot the way

Climbing to the pass

probably was nowhere near strong enough to work properly. In Peray-Tepuy a round and open structure with a conical roof had been built to house the casabe making and they had a large green petrol driven shredding machine from the USA.

Feliciano had toothache but still wanted to comeg so we gave him some of our aspirins. We slept under one of the open thatched huts, but spent a miserable night because of mosquitoes.

Friday 20/11/81,
We set off from Uonori-pá soon after seven with José Luis and Feliciano. Feliciano's little daughter cried and didn't want him to go. José Luis went ahead to hunt and we heard two shots and saw tracks of a danta or tapir, similar in size to a large pig. He eventually returned empty handed. We could see two waterfalls that Feliciano said were Salta Uorchi and Salto Camairan.

We arrived at Uonori-pá (named for the image of a white stork in a rock above the village) about midday. We ate and rested and Steve tried using the cerbatana Feliciano had given him.

It was hot and once we started climbing, we went very slowly as Feliciano

Camp below the pass

Evening meal

wasn't feeling well. Before we reached the plateau, Cecilio caught us up. It is a little alarming to have three Indians as 1,000 B's is all we have to spend and they each want 50 B's a day. However, they all want to come. Cecilia in particular is a law unto himself and enjoys finding the way, but not carrying anything.

The rock looked clean and dry and we wondered if we should change our minds and try the direct route again. But the Indians started cutting a route up and rightwards, aiming for the pass between Ilu Tepui and Kerauren, so we followed. It was slow cutting and walking on tree roots and falling down holes. We reached the 'campamento' in a quebrada by a river about an hour before dark but by the time we had cleared the ground and erected the tent, we were cooking in the dark again. We sat round the fire and shared our supper.

Saturday 21/11/81, en route to pass
It rained an hour or so before dawn and so we cooked and ate breakfast in the confined space of the tent. Everything was muddy and dripping. No one wanted to move till the sun had made a half-hearted attempt at shining. We waited for the rain to clear and began cutting on towards pass.

The way to the top

Camp in the pass

Early morning and we begin the climb

Last night it didn't seem far to the pass but progress is very slow. Today the wall is covered in mist and we are sitting on palm leaves on the sodden ground while the sound of machetes slowly recedes. In a minute, we will move the sacks again. We hope the rain holds off and that we manage to find a decent camp.

Later, after much wandering about, we found a good site – the only dry clearing for miles and bounded on two sides by a clear stream. Cecilio says he came here in the 1950's with a Dr. McGuire who reached the pass but no

Our mattress of bromeliad leaves

Our only source of water

further. We are intrigued and hope to find out who this was when we get back.

Sunday 22/11/81, Climb to pass
Steve and the others cut a path up to the pass while Scharlie has a domestic day in camp.

At about 1 pm we gave up major cutting as the bush had thinned and we pushed on up a bluff dividing the pass into two. It was very steep and we made it to about half way, before retreating. We passed within a few strides of a dark grey snake with lighter cream bands, about 1 metre long. Maybe it was a Bothrops Roraima. We returned to camp as it was getting dark to a good fire and food.

Monday 23/11/81, Camp in pass
Today we retrace our steps with the equipment. We gp right up the centre and the climb is tough. Scharlie kept thinking we should be contouring round to the left but the vegetation was bad enough on the crown of the ridge and looked much thicker in the adjacent quebradas. As Steve said, it was like climbing a compost heap.

We arrived at the top of the cliff adjacent to pass about midday. Looking east we could see Guyana, Quebrada Caco and the headwaters of Mazaruni. José Luis and Cecilio want to go back for casava and they leave us to it. We make camp in the pass, below a long green slope and a rock wall that bars

Struggling up the compost heap

Climbing the first difficult step

the way to the summit.

It is about 5 pm but almost too dark to see. It is wild and windy and thick with mist and we have had to weight the tent down with rocks against the prevailing wind. We chose the flattest driest rocky place to camp but the ground was still soggy so we broke off a sack full of twiggy branches from the heather like bushes and covered them with long leathery bromeliad leaves. This made the most comfortable bed we have had so far. We have collected water for cooking from the bromeliads, the thick leaved pitcher plants that are endemic here.

There is a strong wind and, If the weather stays fair, we are full of hope a bout reaching the summit, maybe tomorrow. The wind means it is difficult to stop the outer tent touching flysheet. Nevertheless, we have a good dry night, and wake to beautiful dawn.

Tuesday 24/11/81, Climb
We woke at dawn as the sky paled behind Kerauren and made its long outline black and sharp. The weather looked fine but the wind was still strong enough to throw you off balance so we stayed warm in the tent till the sun rose then

Crawling under a slab on first step

Surveying the final tower

packed the sacks with ropes and boots, cameras, raisins and warm clothes. Scharlie was wearing two shirts and a fleece it was so cool she kept them on most of the day.

We had decided to take sacks, ropes, rock-boots, and to leave the tent and camping gear, in case there was a chance of getting up in one day. The first stretch from the camp was unexpectedly steep and vegetated. From below the vegetation had looked less dense than the climb to the pass, but the bromeliads were every bit as dense and the patches of scrubby woodland were difficult to push through. We ascended with a strange high stepping roll, crunching and slashing up to our armpits in wet bromeliad.

We began to regret the decision – progress was so slow and we had so far to go that we didn't think we would make it. Still we pushed on, climbing the steepening vegetation, trying always to keep to the crest of the ridge and leaving markers of cut branches and succulents to mark our return in case of mist. We climbed two tree filled gullies where we walked like monkeys on branches only to plunge ignominiously down into the slimy growth below.

Another vegetated slope led us to the first step of the rock wall. We now climbed a further forty feet on rock and vegetated holds. Then a ramp left and a hard move up a wall brought us to the top of a pillar with a narrow chasm the width of a stride between us and a steep rocky section of wall.

We roped up and Scharlie belayed to a block while Steve led up the wall. He was stuck for some time eight feet from the top under a large vegetated overhang. There were two possibilities – a steep, overhanging vegetated

Belaying and bringing up Scharlie

Final pitch

grove, or a delicate traverse left on tiny rounded edges. Without runners, the only way down would be in a fall. Pulling down the overhanging vegetation and mud revealed a good flat ledge about a foot long and two inches deep. Most of the good handholds were now lying in a great sodden mass at the bottom of the pitch. He tried to move left but the Spanish fell boots he was wearing, not very delicate at best, but now caked in mud and goo, slipped off the tiny ripples. Without a decent handhold it was too risky. So back in the overhanging groove he grabbed the remaining vegetation, whipped his left foot into the one good foothold and pushed his right foot as high as possible in the vegetated mass on the right wall of the groove. Miraculously he stayed on and with a final flurry of kicking and slithering, pulled himself up and moved up the groove to tree roots where he could belay Scharlie.

A series of rock steps and more scrambling through bromeliads led to the first step, a rock platform 200 yards metres wide and half a mile long. To reach it we had to step across a deep chasm that caused our hearts to miss a beat. It was sandy and much drier than the pass and we picked out a possible camping place with a view to moving up the next day if we needed more time on the face. The mist was swirling about and the weird black shapes of rock seemed like a maze. We crawled through a rock arch, keeping to the left edge as much

The most difficult pitch of the route

as possible and leaving markers every few metres. Steve cut succulents with the machete and Scharlie built cairns every few metres to help us find our way back if the mist got really bad. We hoped it would lift so that we could at least see a possible route.

Suddenly we came to the end of the plateau and the mist lifted and in front of us we saw a rock castle a hundred feet high, like a sentinel guarding the main rock wall and what was obviously going to be the crux of the route. We skirted the pinnacle on the left and climbed to the gap between the pinnacle and the wall. It was mida-afternoon, but the sky was clear.

The rock wall seemed very steep but a closer look revealed that the area immediately to the right of the prominent roof we had seen from way below was in fact a series of steep, black slabs. Without talking about it we decided to have a go. There was a chance of getting up to the top and it was best to take advantage of the good weather. We could at least leave a fixed rope and return the next day if we failed to get up. We changed into our rock boots and dry socks at the bottom of the wall. We uncoiled the ropes and geared up quickly and Steve began climbing in the middle of the wall at an obvious

Last pitch, Kerauren in background

Ilu Tepui summit, overlooking chasm

niche moving diagonally right.

He climbed the steep black slab on small wrinkles. There were no positive holds and no runners. Stretching right, he reached a difficult step about thirty feet up but failed to make the move since a fall from here would have serious consequences. He traversed five feet left but found it no easier and finally went straight up and moved to a flake and better holds. This led to a wide ledge and chock stone belay in a crack from where he could belay Scharlie while she climbed. (70feet Grade VS 4c)

A few feet left of the belay Steve climbed a crack line to a small pinnacle. He fixed a runner in the crack and moved up to a narrow ledge. He tried moving left up slabs to a loose block about two-foot square surmounting a loose flake. Moving up quickly, he prayed it would stay put when he stepped on it. Unfortunately, after moving up, the holds ran out on a vertical wall and he had to trust his luck stepping down onto the loose block again. He reversed back down to a narrow ledge and traversed twenty feet right on thin lichen covered footholds, pulling the only runner out as he went.

Trending right, steep wrinkled slabs led up to a vegetated ledge. These proved the key to the route. Carefully, testing each handhold because some

Looking south to Kerauren

were loose, he steadily worked his way up these slabs to the grass ledge where he traversed back left until he was above Scharlie and found a block pinnacle belay at the bottom of a steep chimney. Scharlie came up, traversing further right to a corner, before moving up on the slabs. She said she found it hard. (120 feet Grade HVS 5a)

The next pitch led straight up the chimney that Steve climbed direct, bridging between the two sides on small wrinkles. There was a good chockstone at half height, the only good runner on the whole route. (100 ft Grade S 4b)

Two eagles soared above, one in the pass and the other directly above us. We stayed roped but found that the next pitch was only a short easy wall. A gently sloping gully and a scramble up short wall led to the summit blocks where we unroped.

The climb was three hundred feet in all and had taken us about two hours. Quickly we took off our sacks. We left the gear on a slab and walked over to the chimney of the direct route. The sky was clear and the sun warm and we could see across the savannah in Venezuela and the way we had walked.

The wide chimney we had spotted from the bottom and thought we could climb was a great chasm. The mouth was 100 ft. deep and snaked across the plateau to disgorge in the vertical chute of the chimney about 20-30 feet

Looking towards Guyana and the Mazaruni River

wide. The sides were smooth and vertical and the back of the chimney was steep, muddy and covered in green lichen. We couldn't see how vertical it was further down but it looked impossible and we felt we had chosen the best route. Steve persuaded Scharlie to pose on the brink for a photograph.

The top was flat and almost bare of plants, being composed of smooth black slabs of sandstone with small pools of rainwater reflecting the sky. We couldn't decide on the highest point as it always seemed higher wherever we weren't standing so we built several small cairns. North-south the top measured 1,000m while east west it was only a fifth as wide. So the mountain appears widest from Uroy-Uaray and the road while the ridge we had climbed was much narrower.

We took photos and built cairns and went to the Guyanan edge and lay on the rocks and looked down into the jungle of Guyana and the Mazaruni River. It was tempting to stay longer, but it was now late afternoon and we would have to be very quick to get back to the tent before dark.

We wrote a note with our names and the date, and put it in a plastic container under a prominent cairn we built. Then we climbed down to the block belay at the top of the chimney and fixed an abseil, leaving one of our tape slings. One long abseil of 150 ft. reached the chock-stone belay at the

Summit of Ilu Tepuy: Scharlie drinking from a rainwater pool.

top of the first pitch and here we arranged a further abseil directly back to the niche at the start of the first pitch.

The mist held off so we had no problem finding the way across the rock plateau. We crossed the pinnacle and the plateau and arranged a third abseil at the top of the vegetated groove of the first step. That used all the slings we had brought with us. From here, we slid and slipped back down the bromeliads, slithering most of the way and drenching ourselves with muddy water. Following our markers we made it to the tent as the dark was closing in and had just time for a quick wash collecting water from bromeliads for supper. Warm and comfortable, we listened with equanimity to the rain pattering on the tent. We made dinner and Ovaltine by touch in the dark. It rained heavily in the night but we stayed cosy for once. It was much warmer than the previous night.

We had been able to do the climb in the one day because the weather had been perfect and because nothing had gone wrong. The route we had chosen without prospecting the other possibilities was a good way up and gave excellent climbing. The abseils had gone without a hitch and we had had perfect visibility to retrace our steps. Had we waited a day we would have been faced by wet rock.

Into the void

Abseiling back down

More than two people in misty conditions might find it difficult to complete the ascent in one day from the camp on the pass and a higher camp could be made on the plateau before the main wall.

Wednesday 25/11/81, Descent
We have a lazy start to the day watching the dawn from the comfort of our sleeping bags. Steve collects water from the bromeliads and makes tea in bed. We then have a festerous time writing an account of the ascent and start packing up slowly.

We muse on our motives for risking our necks like this. It ought not to be necessary to justify or even explain why we went to climb a mountain in Venezuela but for the fact that so many people asked us the purpose of our trip that a doubt is cast in our minds that perhaps the enterprise or our motivation needs a moment's thought and that an explanation may serve to explain why we go climbing at all and maybe will help us to continue.

Two reasons spring to mind. The first, the desire to confront a challenge, explains why one endures and occasional danger without often getting any real enjoyment. The second, that explains why one goes again, are those rare days of magical ecstasy that leave an insatiable thirst and desire for more.

Venezuelans don't really understand the motivation to climb and, despite our efforts to explain, were never convinced we were doing anything other than searching for gold. We arrived alone with no backup and with little equipment, few clothes and a minimum of food. Our goal was no more developed than a desire to walk through wild country and perhaps to try and

Shampoo

A gelatinous ear-ring

climb an unclimbed peak. This almost arbitrary aim enabled us to travel to remote places one wouldn't otherwise dream of going to and provided the opportunity to get to know people one would never have the chance to meet.

In the past, the principal motives for exploration in Venezuela have been the search for gold, evangelism, and scientific research, especially botany. Our motivation was different. Going to an area where few people have been and climbing a difficult mountain, especially if it is a first ascent, brings a particular kind of satisfaction, a deeper understanding of oneself and the environment in which one travels. Later I found a book by Cesareo de Armellada, a capuchin friar writing in 1960, that addresses this desire for exploration. He writes that the Pemon Indians of the Gran Sabana, when asked what motivates their nomadism, invariably say it is 'esetaká namai'. This translates as a primordial drive to avoid the lifeforce becoming crushed or blocked. They believe that the soul needs a variety of landscape or scenery as the stomach craves a varied diet. (Por la Venezuela Indigena de Ayer y de Hoy, Monografico No. 5, Sociedad de Ciencias Naturales la Salle, Caracas.)

At about ten o'clock there is till no sign of the Indians so we decide to heading down to the campsite in the bog. We begin the long descent, carrying all the equipment and hoping José Luis and Cecilio will come to meet us. Progress was slow and painful – it was wetter and slippy and with the extra weight we were carrying we continually fell into holes.

We descend steeply keeping parallel and to the south side of the quebrada, where we saw the Bothrops Roraima on the way up, and follow the cut path that contours the base of the tequy to our old camp site – the only flat dry

Moss

Lichen

ground in the wide, swampy area with a good river nearby. Tired, hot and muddy we throw of the sacks and sit and take stock. Cecelia and José Luis have left their belongings here so we decide to wait for their return. When they left us on Monday they had said they would go home for more casava and would return the next day. Thinking that we would take two or three days to climb the mountain, we said that we did not need them to return till Thursday or Friday but they had said that they did not want to leave us alone on the mountain so would return on Wednesday, today. However, they seem to have changed their minds.

We bathed deliciously in the stream and had lunch. Steve washed all his clothes so, naked, he was a good target for yhenny. His trousers didn't dry in the sun so he is now singeing them on a clothes-horse he has erected over the fire. Still no Indians, so we get to bed.

Thursday 26/11/81, Unonori-pá
Cecilio and José Luis still hadn't appeared so we decide to continue descending. The only problem is that they have left their tent and together with ours, it is too heavy for us to carry. So we leave it.

From camp, we follow the cut vegetation back towards pass for fifty yards and then a poorly cut path left to the base of the rock wall. After following a path that petered out, maybe Feliiano's return route, we regained the main path that contoured the base of the rock to reach the open quebrada camp site where the Indians had built a roof shelter. From here, the way continued contouring, poor at first, crossing a small stream. Although we ran the risk of

Cutting our way back

Tarantula or 'bird eating' spider

getting lost since the path wasn't that clear, we felt confident we would find our way.

The vegetation changed from dense forest to the more open scrub of the plateau ridge and we reached the main way down to Uanori-Pa. The path follows the plateau due west, descending through forest with various steep sections, and curving to right. After a couple of miles Douglas' old campsite is reached with a good wide quebrada a couple of hundred yards below. We climb steeply from quebrada, past a high rock and then begin crossing a second plateau which is wooded with thick rhododendron-type shrubs and then savannah.

On the descent of the next section we meet Cecilio and Feliciano on their way back up to look for us. They explain that José Luis cut his foot with his machete on the way down, it is infected and he cannot walk. They are pleased and perhaps surprised that we had climbed the mountain and perhaps more particularly that we have managed to get down without an epic that might have involved them. They leave us to continue on down alone while they bash on up to retreive their gear.

On what seems like the home stretch after everything we have been through, after the forest we cross the savannah to the River Uarpa. We wade the river and cross a wood to another river with a log bridge, through another wood, crossing a muddy creek to a savannah and turn south to Uonori-Pa.

We arrive in the village and find that José Luis foot is very swollen and he is in pain up to his groin. He has a high fever and we give him three aspirin to take immediately and eight more, all we have left, to take at four-hourly intervals. Although we haven't had even a graze we realise we have been remiss not bringing a first aid kit and regret no being able to treat him better. We have grown very fond of him and we're very worried for him.

When we arrived at Unonori-pá Feliciano's wife was making cachire, an alcoholic thick, pink liquid is made from yuca and sweet potato, which provides the pink colour. The yuca is masticated by the women and then shredded together with the potato. This mess is then dropped into boiling water in a large pot over an open fire. The liquid is boiled down twice and then sieved and the mass mixed with fresh water to achieve the right consistency.

Feliciano's wife took a number of large gourds and plugged the fine holes in the base of each with sharp sticks that she cut off with a machete. The warm cachire was then transferred to the gourds and they were placed in the river to cool. Later, after Feliciano arrived, they began to drink the cachire, but said it was still sweet and normally needed a couple of days to ferment in the ground before it was ready to drink.

We began to eat that night round the fire. There was a thick casabe and fish soup, picante and casabe bread. It began to rain and we moved under the grass roof of the open hut. José Luis' sister made a fire with dry twigs and the still smouldering logs from the fire outside were transferred under cover.

We continued to eat and Feliciano arrived from the mountain after Cecilio had gone on alone to collect the things he and José Luis had left in the swamp camp. He took off the woven basket on his back, carefully placed his shotgun in the rafters of the hut and produced from a pouch, a small bird he had shot with a china or catapault and threw it to the ground beside his wife.

It was now dark, and the only light was provided by the fire. Feliciano's wife was breast feeding her baby son while Cecilio's baby girl was curled up on a car seat cushion right next to the fire. José Luis' sister took the small bird and began to pluck it.

On the other side of the fire, talking and chatting quietly to José Luis, Feliciano's sister-in-law was teaching his younger sister how to spin cotton.

The whole village of Uroy Uray turns out to say goodbye

She took the bolls from a basket (guayari) at her side. Teasing them in her fingers, she united half-a-dozen into a flat mass which she then teased into a strand about three to four feet long. This she wound round her left fist. Taking a spinning top with her right hand, she unwound a strand of the spun cotton and united this to the unspun strand wound round her hand. Unwinding and pulling this strand out while at the same time twisting the top, the cotton was elongated and then spun rapidly back and forth by twisting between her fingers to form a thread.

Meanwhile, José Luis' sister had finished plucking the bird and with a machete slit its breast open. She carefully took out the bladder, which she threw away, and cleaned the intestines with her thumb and forefinger. She then skewered the bird through its anus with a sharp stick and spread it to roast in front of the flames.

The two babies, Jeyel, Feliciano's year old son, and Ramona's daughter about two years old were sitting between their mothers' outstretched legs. We could hear a loud, dry fluttering sound, like a plastic windmill and realised that the children were playing with live grasshoppers like those we had seen on the way to Roraima. They were about four inches long, had green heads, wings and foreparts and red and black striped abdomens. The children held them by the heads and shook them to make them beat their wings, producing the dry, fluttering sound we had heard. Jeyel played at handing the larger of the grasshoppers to his mother, and then taking it back again. He occasionally popped the brightly striped abdomen into his mouth or pulled off a leg to chew. The game continued for half-an-hour while we ate until the grasshoppers stopped fluttering

Although Feliciano returned last night, we have to wait for Cecilio since he is bringing José Luis' tent and José Luis has our sack locked in his house.

Feliciano spent the morning dismantling and repairing with tools fashioned from files, the shotgun he had bought in Peray Tepuy for 250 Bs he had earned taking Adrian Warren and Don Willans to Kukenan a month or so earlier. The firing mechanism appeared to be faulty and a number of the pieces bent or distorted. He and José Luis worked at fashioning new parts or bending and straightening the existing bits until they got it firing.

Feliciano is fascinated that we managed to climb Ilu Tepui and says he would like to try it too so we give him the ropes as a present. It is hard to leave people with whom one has become friends, knowing you will most probably never see them again.

Friday 27/11/81, Uroy Uruay
Our route back to the road goes through the vegetable patch, then enters the forest crossing three or four small streams to an old clearing. We climb steeply through more forest, cross a stream by the side of enormous log, to savannah and a stony way down a steep hill. The bare red hill and the roof of the school in Uroy Uraiy can be seen in the distance. We cross the Kama by a log bridge to our old camp and finally reach Uroy Uruay where we stay the night.

Saturday 28/11/81, Ciudad Bolivar and Caracas
We were watching a *gavilan* (falcon) chasing parakeets while waiting for a lift when José Luis arrived about 8:30. His foot is bandaged and still very swollen but he is hobbling about now and it should get better. We say good-bye and begin our long journey back to Caracas.

Caracas from Avila

Scharlie looking back at Caracas

Caracas

Wednesday 2/12/81, El Avila Caracas
Just before we left Venezuela Wilmur invited us to go hang-gliding. We assumed he meant to come and watch. He had been talking about it for a while but we had been too busy with our own things to take proper notice and anyway it seemed too improbable.

We drove up the dirt road over the Avila that goes from Cotiza past the Guardia Parques at Los Venados to Boca de Tigre on the summit ridge between Picacho de Galipan and Pico del Avila, the hotel and telepherique. Wilmur unpacked the hang-glider, a pale blue bird. There were plenty of other people getting geared up but Wilmur seemed to be the leader. He came over with a helmet and harness for me and took it for granted I wanted to fly. I said I had never done it before. He said, no problem. It all took a while with me feeling increasingly nervous. I asked what Scharlie would do and how she would get back and he handed her the keys to the Toyota and said she would drive down and collect us on the beach. I had been down this winding dirt road years ago and knew it wasn't straight forward, but Wilmur said someone would go with her and she would be fine.

Wilmur clipped me in and I practiced getting my balance hanging in the control frame. Finally we were ready and Wilmur had me put my arm across his shoulder and under his shoulder strap so we would stay together when we were running. There was a run down a slope and then a drop. I thought I'm going to die. It was against all my built in reflexes to throw myself off a cliff. But I trusted Wilmur. I had never met anyone quite as confident and as genuinely competent in extreme situations. Just before we launched he said don't trip!

We ran down the grass slope and magically we soared into the air. I was hanging behind Wilmur as we rose away from the mountain. Wilmur got me to take over and seemed to disappear behind me. There were huge thunderclouds ahead of us and I gave them a clear berth. I was very gentle and relaxed with my movements. Pushing the bar to the right dipped the left wing and we banked left and vice versa. Pulling the bar made us dive and pushing it away made us rise. I was getting a feel for flight. It was like flying in your dreams, totally silent but for the movement through the air. Magical.

Hang gliding with Wilmur Perez la Riva

Because I had been so cautious and because the day was so thermic we were still thousands of feet up when we arrived over the beach. Wilmur had me do steep turning circles called wingovers. I pushed the bar hard to me right and we flew round in tight steep circles over the sea. He had me fly back inland and suddenly the ground seemed much nearer and there were tall buildings between us and the beach where we were supposed to land. Wilmur nudged me aside and flew between the towers and lined up for the beach. It was all happening so fast. We seemed to be hurtling towards the beach and for the second time I thought I was going to die. I couldn't imagine how we were going to land without crashing and smashing ourselves. But from flying along in a prone position Wilmur flared the wing up, we stalled and dropped to our feet with a little plop. It was incredible, I could not believe it. I unclipped from the glider, walked to the shade of a sea grape and sat on its gnarled roots and contemplated my deliverance. I was drained and elated at the same time.

A while later Scharlie arrived, equally euphoric have negotiated the long steep mountain road and found her way to the beach in a jeep she had never driven before. We have to do this when we get back I said. It's just fantastic.

Notes about the trip

Gran Sabana

The Gran Sabana is part of a region known as the Guyanan Shield that extends from the Talfenberg in Surinam west to the Sierra Macarena in Colombia and from the Orinoco in the north to the Rio Branco, Brazil in the south. The most notable feature of the region are the 2-3,000 metre table mountains of the Roraima series known as tepuy in Pemon and Jidi in Yekuana the language of the Makiritare. Much of the mythology of indigenous groups involves stories about these mountains.

    Rising out of the surrounding grassland and forest, the Tepui are the eroded remains of the Caledonian Sea bed and are composed of sheer blocks of sandstone or quartzite, geologically the oldest rocks on earth. The rock is generally hard, being of a similar consistency to millstone grit, or it would not have resisted the erosion of millions of years.

    Tepuis tend to be found as isolated entities rather than in connected ranges, which makes them the host to a unique array of endemic plant and animal species. Of these, Roraima, on the border with Guyana and Brazil, and the Auyan-Tepuy, over which Angel Falls, the highest waterfall in the world tumbles, are the most famous.

    Rain clouds build up as the heat of the day evaporates the sodden vegetation at the base of the mountains and the tops are usually swathed in mist. Sudden, short-lived rainstorms move across the savannah like transparent curtains, the rain slanting down in psychedelic lines as the light from the sun is broken by the raindrops.

    There is little vegetation on the tops of the mountains and when it rains, the water courses over the black slabs and into deep chasms to fall over the edge thousands of feet to the jungle below. The savannah is criss-crossed by many crystal clear streams, and rivers that flow eventually into the Caroni which feeds the majestic Orinoco.

Indian culture

The Indians we got to know as friends. They treated us as guests in their home. They fed us royally on fish, fish soup, picante, casabe, bananas, and allowed us into the daily activities of their life. They were intelligent, strong, honourable and attentive. They seemed much more content and self-assured than they had ten years ago. They are completely at home in this environment. They appreciate clearly the differences in their life-style and don't envy people living in cities.

The whole area is almost completely uninhabited. Between El Dorado, a small settlement around a penal colony in the north, and Santa Elena, a small town clustered around a Silesian mission on the Brazilian border, there is a Venezuelan army encampment, a further mission and a number of small indigenous settlements of Taurepan Indians.

These Indians, descendants of the warrior Caribe, live a semi-nomadic existence, never content to stay long in their rude wattle and daub homes. They vary their lives by switching continually from tending established plantations to moving to temporary hunting encampments or visiting relatives in other settlements.

Uroy-Uaray, our sort of base for the expedition, is a small Taurepan settlement on the main dirt road through the Gran Sabana at a point where it is crossed by a good wide river. Nearly a dozen homes are randomly dispersed around a school-cum-Adventist chapel that suggests the reason for the village's existence.

The first time we arrived in Uroy-Uaray, the village seemed full of people. A dozen or so men were sitting or lounging against the wall of the half-complete school-master's house, waiting for a lift to Santa Elena to go mining for a week or so. Ramon had escorted us here to see if anyone was prepared to guide us to Ilu-Tepuy and here we met José Luis. At first sight, he wasn't as impressive as Ramon, being shorter and of slighter build and much less confident of manner. However, over the following weeks, he was to prove a humorous and loyal companion and a tower of strength, cutting a path through the tangled jungle at the base of the mountain.

Equipment and food

The choice of what equipment and food to take on an expedition like this is obviously a matter of personal preference. Since we had no car, we travelled as light as possible, carrying (apart from ropes which José Luis carried) all the gear and food for two weeks packed in relatively small Berghaus Munroe rucksacks which proved ideal.

This desire to travel light, governed most of our decisions. Firstly, how to camp. Ideally one would, in the lowest camps, sleep in hammocks with mosquito nets under a communal tarpaulin and have a tent for the high camp above the tree line. Since it rained most nights and it was important to sleep warm and dry before making an attempt on the upper wall, we decided to take a light two-man tent (Saunders GC2) and dispense with the luxury of hammocks in the lower camps.

This plan worked, but had hammocks and tarpaulin been available, it would have been worth taking them since one of the Indians would have carried the extra load without difficulty. Scharlie's hollowfill sleeping bag dried much quicker than my old down bag, but was more bulky. We had fitted long zips to both so we could unzip them when we got hot.

We took only the clothes we stood in, jeans and a long sleeved cotton shirt, plus old polar fleece jackets for the nights. Since we could wash in streams and dry out quickly in the sun we didn't miss having a change, except returning on the bus. However, an old pair of silk pyjamas to change into at night would have been lovely. For footwear, we went for maximum comfort since we had so far to walk –We walked over three hundred miles in the five weeks we spent in the Gran Sabana. Scharlie chose trainers and I used Spanish Fell boots with canvas uppers. Both were fine.

As regards climbing gear, we took two 9 mm ropes, rock boots, five nut runners on wires and four tapes. Since there was only one good runner on the whole route we could have done without the nuts. We dispensed with a harness and roped up the old fashioned way, with a bowline knot round our waists. For the abseils we used slings and figure-of-eight descenders. Three of the four tape slings were left on the abseils.

In the lower camps, we contrived to make a fire both to cook on and for light and warmth. The essential equipment for making fire was a sharp machete and a file to sharpen the machete. We used a stick lighter and had matches in a film container in case this got lost. A flint might have been more useful. We became adept at making a fire, even in wet conditions, by cutting away the damp outer part of logs and by building the fire so that wood could be dried above the hot burning centre. However, we never got as good as the Indians who could get a fire going under an improvised palm leaf roof in a rainstorm. We took a gaz stove and two canisters for wet conditions, quick starts in the morning and for the high camps. By mainly using fires we used a cylinder a week.

We ate out of the pan and drank from the empty plastic date container. We had a penknife and a spoon each. These later were a continual source of tension since one was noticeably bigger than the other.

Our diet was limited, both by what we could carry and what could be obtained in Caracas. Breakfast was invariably hot porridge, milk made for excellent creamy milk powder and brown sugar scraped from a block of cane sugar called pabellon. Evening meals were made from packet soup with pasta or instant rice, plus sardines, tuna or corned beef. Additional luxuries were dates, raisins and boiled sweets and tea bags. The Indians had casabe, the flat round bread made from yuca, and hot pepper sauce in a small bottle. We shared our porridge and stews with them into which they dipped casabe.

After two or three weeks, we began to tire of the packet soup flavour of evening meals. But considering the limitations on weight, we ate well. Staying such a long period in the same area with the same small group of people, we made close friends and on returning to their homes we were feasted. On arrival we would be given bananas then after an interlude fish soup, hot pepper sauce, casabe soup, small fish and casabe bread would be put in front of us. A communal bowl of cachire, the pink, alcoholic drink would then be passed around. These breaks in our monotonous diet naturally made all the difference. Although both José and Feliciano carried shotguns, they never managed to bag anything and they felt the lack of variety in their diet as well. After getting us to the pass, they went back to Uonori-Pa to get more food.

Water was not a problem. There are many crystal-clear streams and rivers and we did not carry water with us. However, a light folding water container, like a small canvas bucket might have been useful, especially in the camp on the pass, where we had to collect water from bromeliads and filter it through a clean pair of Scharlie's knickers, and in a lower camp on the ridge where we collected water from a hole dug in the ground.

Things usually taken on expeditions that we didn't miss included a torch, mugs, a watch, binoculars and books. We went to bed when it got dark and woke with the dawn, and we learned to tell the time remarkably accurately, or so we believed, by the position of the sun.

Things we omitted to take and did miss included: a first aid kit – especially iodine, antiseptic cream, band-aid and more asprin, a belt – with the loss in weight, trousers begin to fall down and sun glasses. Scharlie also ran out of writing paper. Although we didn't get lost, a compass might have helped in dense undergrowth.

A mosquito net would also have been very useful, especially when sleeping in the Indian villages. Some areas were especially plagued by sandflies during the day and mosquitos at night, although at different times the same areas might be free. We didn't discover any real pattern except that a strong breeze kept the sandflies away and that the mosquitos were especially bad immediately after rain, or even during a rainstorm, if we were under cover

Transport
We flew from London to Caracas. From the airport in Marquetia a bus goes to Parque Central in Caracas. From here it was only a short walk to the bus terminal in Nuevo Circo. There was no bus all the way to the Gran Sabana, but a daily one got to Tumeremo leaving 6.30 pm and arriving 9 am and from here a jeep or mini-bus could be taken. The return journey was similar and other buses are available from Callao, Upata and Pto Ordaz, other towns on the same road back to Caracas.

www.ingramcontent.com/pod-product-compliance
Lightning Source LLC
Chambersburg PA
CBHW042327150426
43193CB00001B/13